# Action Art

# Sculpting

## Isabel Thomas

## www.raintreepublishers.co.uk

Visit our website to find out more information about **Raintree** books.

To order:
- ☎ Phone 44 (0) 1865 888112
- 📄 Send a fax to 44 (0) 1865 314091
- 💻 Visit the Raintree Bookshop at **www.raintreepublishers.co.uk** to browse our catalogue and order online.

First published in Great Britain by Raintree,
Halley Court, Jordan Hill, Oxford OX2 8EJ,
part of Harcourt Education.
Raintree is a registered trademark of Harcourt
Education Ltd.

Editorial: Melanie Copland, Kate Buckingham
and Lucy Beevor
Design: Jo Malivoire and AMR
Picture Research: Mica Brancic
Production: Duncan Gilbert
Originated by Modern Age
Printed and bound in China by South China
Printing Company.

ISBN 1 844 21241 6 (paperback)
09 08 07 06 05
10 9 8 7 6 5 4 3 2 1

**British Library Cataloguing in Publication Data**
Thomas, Isabel
Sculpting – (Action Art)
730
A full catalogue record for this book is available
from the British Library.

**Acknowledgements**
Corbis pp. **13**, **15**; Getty p. **4**; Harcourt Education
p. **14** (Gareth Boden) p. **11** (Martin Sookias) p. **6**
(Trevor Clifford), pp. **5**, **8**, **9**, **10**, **12**, **16**, **18**, **19**,
**20**, **21**, **22**, **23**, **24** (Tudor Photography); Topfoto
pp. **7**, **17** (The Image Works)

Cover photograph of boy making a clay
helicopter reproduced with permission of
Corbis/Gallo Images (Anthony Bannister)

Every effort has been made to contact copyright
holders of any material reproduced in this book.
Any omissions will be rectified in subsequent
printings if notice is given to the publishers.

The paper used to print this book comes from
sustainable resources.

**Disclaimer**
All the Internet addresses (URLs) given in this
book were valid at the time of going to press.
However, due to the dynamic nature of the
Internet, some addresses may have changed, or
sites may have changed or ceased to exist since
publication. While the author and publishers
regret any inconvenience this may cause readers,
no responsibility for any such changes can be
accepted by either the author or the publishers.

Some words are shown in bold, **like this**. You can find them in the glossary on page 23.

# Contents

# What is art?

Art is something you make when you are being **creative**.

People like to look at art.

A person who makes art is called an artist.

You can be an artist too!

# How can
# I make art?

There are lots of ways to make art.

You can draw and paint pictures.

Try making sculptures and collage with interesting **textures**.

# What are sculptures?

Sculptures are not flat like paintings and drawings.

They are **three-dimensional**.

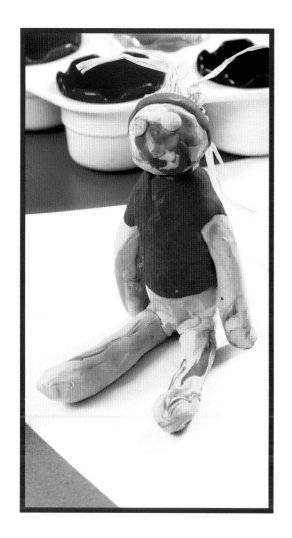 

Each side of a sculpture
looks different.

# What can I use to make sculptures?

straws

shiny foil

string

paper

Look at all the **materials** you can use for sculpting.

glue

Build a model by joining things
together with glue or sticky tape.

# How can I make clay and sand sculptures?

Clay is soft and squishy.

Squeeze it into shapes or roll it into strips.

Sculpting with wet sand is fun.

**Decorate** your sand sculptures with shells and pebbles.

# How can I make paper and card sculptures?

You can make a model of a cow with a box.

Draw eyes and a nose on your model.

dinosaur

Use **papier mache** to make a dinosaur.

When your dinosaur is dry, you can paint it.

15

# What can I sculpt?

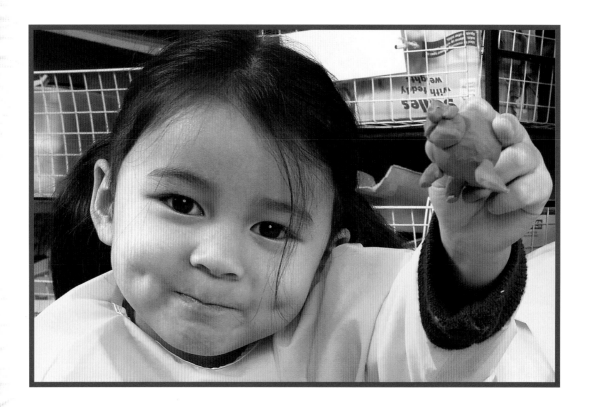

You can make a sculpture of something real, like an animal.

You can invent a shape that is interesting to look at.

# How does sculpting make me feel?

It is fun to make art with other people.

Help each other to build a big sculpture.

18

When you finish making a sculpture, you feel pleased.

# Let's make a sculpture!

Let's make a sculpture of a tree!

1. Ask a grown-up to help you collect some leaves and twigs.

2. Roll out a thick piece of clay to make the trunk. Stand it up on a board.

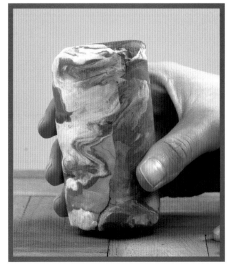

3. Use your fingers to make marks in the clay.

Try to make a rough **texture**, like tree bark.

4. Stick twigs and leaves into the top of the trunk.

# Quiz

All these **materials** are used for sculpting.

Can you remember what they are called?

Look for the answers on page 24.

# Glossary

 **creative**  making something using your own ideas and how you feel inside

 **decorate**  add colours and patterns to make something look nice

 **materials**  things you use to make sculptures, like paper and clay

 **papier mache** material made of paper soaked in water and mixed with glue

 **texture**  how something feels when you touch it

 **three-dimensional**  shape that is not flat, like a bottle

# Index

Answers to quiz on page 22

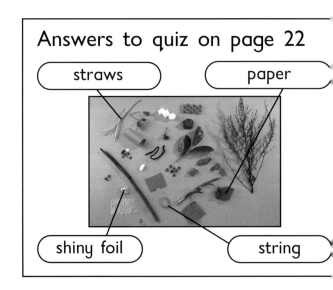

straws

paper

shiny foil

string

24